The Offering

The Offering

poems by

Eleanor Kedney

Liquid Light Press
Premium Chapbook First Edition
Copyright © 2016

ISBN-10: 0-9909267-8-8

ISBN-13: 978-0-9909267-8-8

Liquid Light Press

poetry for the heart

www.liquidlightpress.com

Book design: M. D. Friedman
Cover & Author Photos: Peter D. Schaffer

for my mother, Helen,

who loved to dance

Contents

The Offering

Driving from Shoshone to Pahrump,
I hit a female quail.
I set her still body
on the side of the road.
As darkness descends on her eggs,
her mate will call for her.

Daybreak, I fill a basin with water,
and the Gambel's Quail gather.
Males with full top-knots
and red-brown crowns
scamper among the covey of twenty.
Like Cézanne's *Bathers*,
plump, pear-shaped bodies
circle in merriment, bright sun
chasing their shadows.

My Brother Pruning the Sweet Gum Tree

My brother was six feet tall and tan,
pruning the sweet gum tree he planted
on the porch side of the house. His blue
jeans hung loose on his hips; his
bare chest heaved as he sucked in smoke,
Marlboro Man style, the cigarette hanging
from his lips, his ribs ready to burst
through skin as he jumped up and grabbed
a branch. Callused hands stained
by the dried burgundy sap of trees
he cut, leaves he stripped, shredded
between fingers that could break
a limb—fingers doubled in size—thick
from hard work. He released the branch
and it snapped back. He was quick,
maybe high, his body, uncomfortable
next to mine, pivoted in and out of the shadows,
scarred arms reaching beyond himself.
I watched the sweat mix with dirt,
drip down his face, his curly hair tangled
on the back of his neck. His eyes,
small in their sockets, fixed on me
as he grabbed another branch and pointed
to the flared stems that suck life from the tree.
In a low mumble from years of alcohol,
he said it would be my job when he was gone
to prune the tree, to do just this.
That fall his organs shut down, and I can't
prune that damn tree, still coming back
to life, more full, every spring.

Reading Frank O'Hara after My Mother's Death

I buy an *Arizona Daily Star* to read obituaries
in which everyone was kind, generous, and will be missed.
The advice given from a heart doctor:
Don't look at the stat monitors;
you can't live by the numbers.
There were days hers were so good.
This month, a blue moon on New Year's Eve.
The maid at the Waldorf, a Russian Jew, told me,
Get out and walk. Don't look at anybody,
don't go into stores, just walk.
In St. Bartholomew's church,
a woman turned to a man—
God wants you to live as long as possible.
I just wanted quiet.
The kind of quiet that comes out of stillness:
hummingbird wings sculling the air;
Ave Maria sung as liturgy by an opera singer.
I took a wrong turn today up the mountain.
Now, I wear blue topaz, the color of my mother's eyes,
oval stones in a bracelet, hoop earrings.
Though I am not mineral or vitreous
I have been touched, turned, warmed, and cut.
I want to believe that the dog lick-kisses my lips
because she loves me and not
for the sweet jam in the corners of my mouth.
Now, I count lights when I drive,
snack instead of eat meals.
Now, the wave of a bare greasewood in the wind,
the orange flowers that hang on
the Cape honeysuckle in January amaze me.

What We Do

He tells me I will never be alone.
I hold him before he leaves the bed. He holds
my hand when we are lying there talking.
He rubs between the shoulder blades
where grief is held in my body.
I give him head pets, scalp massages
when he can't fall asleep, even if I am tired.
If I cook eggs, I give him the unbroken ones.
He walks the dog, takes out the garbage and the recycling.
Often I'll do the dishes, even if it's not my turn.
He takes care of all the bills.
I do the food shopping, house cleaning,
launder the towels and sheets.
He doesn't understand my connection to rocks
but lets me bring them into the house.
I bought him his menorah, light the candles with him,
and learned to make the matzo ball soup.
I remind him to call his father.
He loves the dog and all animals.
He is with me when I cry in the middle of the night.
I love him every day. I tell him
he is handsome. I tell him I'll be there
for him when his father dies.
I get up to see him off to work
making sure he has some fruit to take with him.
I show him the yellow caterpillar
I hold in my palm that will turn
into a Hummingbird Moth.
He is sensitive to the sacredness of life.
I read him this poem.
He canceled business trips, conference calls,
and left work early to be with me.
I take care of him when he is well and sick.

He drives me back and forth to the hospital
at night when I am exhausted.
I gave him a scuba diving course as a gift
so he will be safe in the water.
He is patient with my OCD, puts up with my impatience
and messiness. I encourage him to sing
telling him he has a good voice.
I talk through my dreams.
He helped with the memorial, doing whatever I needed.
I went to his doctor's appointments
when his retina was torn.
He stopped working out to be at the hospital
or to come home and be with me.
He calls every day to check in with me
the way my dad did with my mom.
I make snack bags for us to take on the airplane.
He tries to make me laugh with silly clichés.
I check in with him if he doesn't
call me, the way my mom did with my dad.
We'll take care of each other when we are old.
I root for the Patriots with him and make guacamole.
He gave me the best birthday card ever.
We lie on the floor with the dog.
We ride a bicycle built for two.
He walks on the street side of the sidewalk
to protect me like his grandmother taught him to do.
He told my mom, as he did my dad,
he would always take care of me.
He'll marry me again.
I only swim with *him*.

Between the Earth and Sky

Though we stayed until dark you died alone in the hum of a white room.

The priest's odd laugh at your burial as I held hard dirt in my fist.

Gasoline is what Tony said you drank on a dare in a shit bar.

Leaving the Bronx hospital at night was dangerous but I did it.

A rush of junkies at the wake shaking for a fix shook hands with Dad.

Methadone clinics are disguised gray buildings between the earth and sky.

Outside the methadone clinic a guy tried to sell you heroin.

With plates pulled off we abandoned your broken truck on an unswept street.

Your body in plastic beyond a window for claiming and naming.

The sweet gum you planted is tall and leafing and breathing and bleeds sap.

Memories of My Father

Churlish leaves kick up.

Some gather, some scatter, some are latched

in the hemlock tree, a few lie

tucked between the white slats of fence.

I rake and they reappear.

Brown-edged, curled like cupped hands begging.

I bag them, tie it shut.

But there are always more. They scrape,

brittle-scuttle across the steps,

wind giving them a voice.

Shades

My mother was sixteen when her mother died—
her body laid out in the parlor.
The shades were drawn, marking the house
of the dead. People came to the wake
bringing homemade cakes and bottles
of brown liquor.

By the time I was sixteen, my mother buried
four sisters and four brothers.
When the last died, she stayed up all night
drinking beer with ice cubes, smoking
Kent Lights in the dark, the Zenith TV blinking.
The drawn shades, darkened by nicotine,
thin and papery as dead moth wings,
outside, stars extinguished like embers.

Desert Spiny Lizard

Blue-green throat, dark collar,
keeled scales faintly fluorescent.
In my palm it moved its head slowly
as though roused from deep slumber
and not the moment before death.
I nestled it behind sage, flaring against rock.
The next morning it was gone,
ran off, I believed, to eat ants and spiders.
Later, outside my door, camouflaged
on gravel, black eyes fixed
beneath pearl-gray lids. I waited
a long time, warm hands cupped.
When my mother's eyelids closed
and her breathing stopped, I held her
with nothing left to try. I buried the lizard
just two inches below ground;
next spring, the weather warm, it might crawl
out of the earth.

Fiftieth Birthday

A muggy June afternoon——Dad had shore
leave——we took a bus to watch you play.
Your fastball dazed the best batters
and dazzled Daddy, too. I huddled next to him
in the bleachers, but all eyes were on you,
everyone yelling, *C'mon Pete.*
Strike one, two, then three, another inning yours.
I tugged on Daddy's shirt, bent the fingers back
on his left hand, saying, *Daddy, take me for ice cream.*
The ice cream was purple, and it was just Dad
and me eating two scoops on a cake cone.
The sounds of the game grew distant;
the floodlights on the field came on and lit
up the sky.

Now I wonder what it was like for you
to hear the crowd cheering,
to look up into the stands for the only man
who mattered and not see him there.

I woke this morning, surprised to be 50.
It's been 16 years since we stood in the wind-whip
on Saint Mary's Hill and buried you.
I didn't know that I would be the one
not at rest, strong-armed by old hurts,
imagining you a protector from the past
that forgives no one.

Twelve Days from Transfer

Because they suppress you with Lupron & that's the easy-to-mix
shot, the cheapest shot, the thinnest diabetic's needle that goes
into the soft part of the belly, hell, that one you can give
to yourself with a running start, in airport bathrooms, friends'
bedrooms, wherever you're going, this one won't slow you down
on day 21.

Because 50% of follicles contain an egg, they build you up
with Metrodin, FSH, 30-40 amps per cycle, $2,000
of the $12,000 you'll spend & this is where you need to totally trust
someone to break the glass ampoules & mix the white tablets
with 2 cc's of saline & clear the syringes of air bubbles
without losing even a drop, to put their hand on your butt
in the shape of an "L" & find the corner of skin where your top
pocket would be so they don't hit a nerve & inject the 1½-inch
needle into the muscle.

They tell you not to worry, the symptoms are temporary,
you take the headaches, hot flashes, vaginal dryness, bruising
at the injection site, abdominal bloating, breast tenderness,
moodiness & irritability.

Because they check you every other morning, then every morning
at 7:30 a.m., take blood, do a vaginal ultrasound & you see
your follicles like black pools on a screen, mapped by *x's*,
intern of the day calling out the numbers to record on a sheet
until there are some 13 on the left ovary & at least 10 on the right,
over 18 mm averages & he'll smile as he says, *Tonight might be
the night* & you actually look forward to HCG, Profasi
or Pregnyl, the toughest shot for side effects, but he says,
We'll call you when we have your estradiol.

HCG matures follicles, retrieval is 34 hours after injection
& Dr. Jones, IVF clinic, does a transvaginal oocyte
aspiration using a probe attached to a suction pump & they get
nine eggs, great for a 41-year-old woman.

Because they give you the dish from the embryos
as a souvenir & you see them on the screen, their cells
divided so they are no longer zygotes, their outer shell
intact, they all look good, perfect gray moons & you want
to name them, lying there on the table, rolling dice
in your mind, *OK, let's put in six.*

Because they support you with progesterone suppositories
& Estraderm patches, the lining of your uterus builds
& you become full, there is no other way to explain it & in 12 days
you know if you're pregnant.

Twelve days is a long time to wait & you don't
want the lab to take blood anymore, nick your hemorrhagic
veins, wait for estradiol levels or follicular sizes
& the speculations of the best doctors as to what
is your next best shot & you don't want to open
your legs for the vaginal ultrasound microphone
covered by a rubber & cold, sea-green gel before
you even have your breakfast, have sex on the right day,
at the right hour, whether you want to or not, be home
at 7:00 p.m. to pull down your pants & Jesus
to talk about it or try this again.

Good to See You

In front of Saks at Christmas,
watching synchronized snowflakes blinking
in dark windows
to "Carol of the Bells,"
I could live again for the penny
found on the ground.

My mother died,
and after forty days and forty nights
I blend green vegetables
to get vitamins
quickly into my bloodstream.
I've never smoked a banana peel
but I received communion
when I wasn't in a state of grace.

Daily I erase regret.
It gives me pleasure to agree.
A rule I've adopted is to listen
but not give anyone advice.
Twice, I fluttered my eyes.

I've learned to say, *Good
to see you,* instead of, *How
are you?* so as not to hear
dredged up miseries or refrains.
I have a plugged up salivary gland,
but no one wants to look in my mouth.

Now I write short sentences
joined by semicolons. I'm not a whale;
I'm not Jonah; I'm not that epic.

Ajoite in Quartz

Rough-edged, hard as knuckle.

Bottom indented like a palm—

the stria a short, broken lifeline.

Rock cut from larger rock, I remember

the hand of my older brother

holding mine to cross the busy road.

Cold at first, slowly becoming warm.

I bring you to my lips, smell earth, run

my thumb along the yellow-brown

like flesh stained by nicotine.

Ajoite, mineral in milky quartz,

blue-green veins in soft pink, deep within,

pink of muscle, alive with memory—

my brother, addicted to heroin,

yanking me back to the curb.

At the Cemetery

The Christmas carnations

on my mother's headstone

have laid their brown heads down.

I clear the snow off her name.

A row away, an old man

must have heard me.

A cap in his hand, he says,

Don't cry, she's at peace,

no rent, no cooking.

On the hill, the old elm

wrapped in ice, hangs low.

Such cold, and a long white sky.

Twigs break beneath my feet.

Love Poem

The rabbit's eye——placid, dark,
beholding as I walked the dog
along the fence where it sat,
plump, anchored in its body,
gray fur brushed by a wintry breeze.

After midnight, I offered lettuce
and from the dark watched it eat.
The wind moved on, the settlement of stars, calm.

At light's first glance I saw the rabbit
lying on its side——eyes open, ears back,
the crown of its head settled into a notch in a tree.
Legs felled straight, its face without pain.
Beauty so plain consoled me.

Rain came, seemed like old rain:
emptying the sky, washing down dust.

Childless

Three young coyotes pause
under the palo verde.
A woman sits nearby

watching light fade beyond
the mountains.
Today her friend said,

*It is really something to watch
your child do anything.*
She rears her heart in the desert:

harsh needles and striking
blooms, endless
sky, big sun.

Less lonely around animals
than people, she remains
so the pack will stay.

They play the way boys play
to test their strength,
crashing against the tree.

Stars emerge in their cool
blue silence.

Apple Pie

I found my father sifting,
fine white flour falling into drifts
in the belly of a yellow bowl.
While he turned the crank
and metal moved like a scythe
scraping against mesh, he was quiet,
young in natural light,
his cheeks ruddy, his dark hair
slick with Brylcreem, combed high,
the tip of his tongue on his lower lip
as when he wrote Christmas cards,
marking extra dots above *i's,* adding
curlicues to the tails of *g's* and *y's.*
I wanted to know his thoughts.
The Cortland apples, peeled and cored
while I had slept, waited on the counter
dressed in cinnamon and sugar as if this
was a special occasion, though
he often made pie early in the morning
—pie pleased and his inspired praise.
He'd serve me a piece complete with swirls
of whipped cream and look into my face.
He was a kid that way. I didn't pretend
I could someday make pie and it would taste like his——

the crust flaking when it hits the tongue,

the apples spicy-sweet and buttery, but sleepily

I listened to what he wanted to tell me

about measuring Crisco and chilling dough.

He had no written recipe, only his ease

cutting in shortening, his wrist moving back

and forth as if rocking a cradle.

Big fingers handled dough like delicate fabric,

easing it into a pie plate, fluting the crusts

with his thumb, his mark. He set the timer

and it loudly ticked away our minutes.

The morning of his wake, my mother threw away

the last piece of apple pie to make room

for cold cuts, salads, and sodas.

I lifted it out of the garbage and ate it.

Shoes

How life starts with those first shoes, sponged white & saved
in a clear box or bronzed on a platform, little girls
in calfskin, kidskin, patent leathers for making First Communion,
shined with Vaseline, buckled down, the white & brown
saddle shoes of Catholic schools, Buster Browns, Stride Rites,
penny loafers with nickels slipped in; the tasseled, the tied, the wide
wingtips of Wall Street, the King's blue suede shoes,
snakeskin, man-made uppers & rubber soles, old shoes with holes
in soles, can't seem to throw them away, Keds for baby boomer
women seeing themselves in ads, affording designer shoes,
expensive even-on-sale Via Spiga shoes, Donald J. Pliner
shoes handmade in the mountains of Italy; got to have
the walking shoe, the airport shoe, the shoe to slip off
during lovemaking, those red shoes
& the squeaky shoes that say you're arriving, that say you're leaving;
there are shoes that sell cars & shoes that say you're practical,
there are the shoes of stories——
stilettos filled with champagne,
satin & lace-covered fabric shoes dyed to match the dress
& glass slippers that disappear at midnight, ruby slippers
that bring you home, shoes you don't take off; shoes to walk
the dog in, jog in, new ones to break in, give you rhythm
& shoes that make you tall,
tricolored platform shoes looking good with tight jeans, shoes
that go with fashion & shoes that make you punk, Greenwich Village
cafe boots imitating army issue,
or the thick shoes of the oppressed in Russia;
shoes to polka as fast as you can, get a grip in, the Kinney shoes
Dad tap-danced in, that made us kids laugh,

shoes Gene sang & danced in the rain in, *Riverdance*—
the sound of a cast of shoes
rapping hard on wooden floors, clapping for more, moving our feet,
the sound of the one-heartbeat, an uncle, a cop, walking the beat,
marching feet in unison, never-out-of-step beat, toe the line
stride in Florsheims; rubber-thonged, happy feet, Dunhams
covered in mud, closed-toed shoes to walk through puddles in,
slingbacks you're not supposed to walk in puddles with,
Totes to keep the water out, lead boots people have drowned in,
the only pair of new shoes he owned (to bury my brother in);
worn thrift store shoes, markdowns, hand-me-downs,
first pair of heels worn to church, feeling like a big girl
though-my-feet-ache shoes, white go-go boots, singing
along with Nancy, *Gonna walk all over you,*
the old woman who didn't really live in a shoe;
shoes that point, that have a steel toe, 5 ½—my size,
grandpa's prize-fighting dodging shoes; don't have the right shoes,
the shoes that match, don't match, kids in India without shoes,
Jellies for the beach, sand in shoes, "made in America"
billboard shoes that didn't last, orthopedic shoes,
extra-wide-width shoes, old lady shoes & widow Red Cross shoes,
time & time again the empty shoes, the hollows
filled with shoe trees or ecru paper, the thrown-away shoe,
the mud-caked, left-on-the-riverbank shoes, the army issue
of the unknown soldier, the one shoe lost under the bed;
my new black boots, better than any shoes,
like the spit-shined Navy boots my father wore,
his coming-home boots, tight-on-the-heel boots,
felt them with my whole body pulling, slip off
to the floor.

Tomatoes

Spring. My father would buy tomato plants, tall ones

given a head start at a nursery, picking varieties with promise:

Big Boys and Beefsteak. The first ripe and heavy fruit dropped

into his thick hands were a feast of sandwiches

on white bread with mayonnaise. In the early evening, he'd give

tomatoes to anyone who walked by. Listened to strangers.

His sober best was about love. After he died, neighbors said

he made time for them. I came to understand the man, home

after twenty-seven years in the Navy, who moved about the kitchen

cooking roasts, simmering brown gravy, rolling dough for pies

in silence, and holding cartons filled with tomatoes

as though they were his sweet prodigies.

Desert Millipede

After a monsoon, I lift a millipede
on a stick, watch it coil,
expose only its armored side.
For twenty years, I've tried to grieve
for my brother. After his death,
I tried to write a poem. About running
into an old friend of his, off drugs
and doing well. About a young man
in New York City, well-dressed
in a tweed coat, with wavy brown hair,
collapsed in a pharmacy doorway,
seeing my brother's face in his,
and not being able to look away.
About my brother's first day home
from prison, and how he stood boastful
in the shabby light of our parents' living room.
About my brother as a boy who couldn't play
with toys without breaking them.
About the phone calls that kept coming
for him, and I couldn't admit
he died from an overdose, and lied.
I put the millipede down and it uncurls,
even though vulnerable in the light.
It moves in a wave, some legs
always touching the ground.

Old Man in a Drugstore Parking Lot

He told the threadbare joke how Van Nuys
got its name, like we were chums who once
sat on a stoop, shared peanuts in shell,
and knew an old woman or two who
closed their windows at four, slid curtains
against the coming nightfall. His hand
tapped my arm and begged the vacant air
as he tried to remember where his
daughter lived: Colorado, California,
or maybe *my* town. The sky became
muddled with sprays of snow, black ice formed
on Stonington Road, the long drive flecked
by how I dismissed his delight. There
were yellow truck lights to follow home,
silver guard rails twisted in half-moon
angles along turns. That night, lying
alone, the windows without curtains,
sycamores leaning their elbows in,
the church bell marking each passing hour,
I thought of my father handing me
apple pie, followed by a tap dance.

After a Death, I Take a Walk

The cactus wren trumpets its call,
Come here, dear, come here.
The sun is rising gently,
staghorn spines soften in silver light,
and the angular face and sloped back
of the Catalina Mountains slumber in shadow.

The dog leads me into the wash
to the remains of a quail eaten in the night,
a pile of feathers. The scent holds her.

The cactus wren, alert with pleasure,
lures us back toward the house.
It's good to linger in the cool swells of wind,
smelling new leaves, green on the desert willow,
before the day's heat declares itself,
and the ungroomed silences pass
between the living.

A Long Period of Sadness

Wind pushes the edges of my house.

It curls a fan dance, murmurs

close to the ear, sweeps down my neck.

Inside, there's solace

in peeled oranges, softened cheese.

Soon, the moon drops,

seeds blow in from a distance.

The wind is a dangerous thing,

knocking at the screen door.

Hurls itself sure-shot and rock-heavy.

It doesn't say, *yes*, it says, *no*,

throaty and hollow. My palms press

against the window, feels like an echo:

no more. The sky tumbles and brightens.

Inside there's been solace in canned goods,

pan-fry, thick slices of cornbread.

Soon, tossed fruit drops, the calling

of my name stops—released

from what failed to bloom.

Movement

Among rock and gravel
an angling, bare ocotillo
leafs and flowers—
red flame tips torch the sky.

Outside, clouds roam
and quail chitter on the gate.
Everything bidden by the sun has risen.
Among spines of staghorn—
fruit and flowers and seeds.

Fallow beyond spring,
I read of the night movements
of green plants folding in
then opening at dawn.
I push memory's mulch aside
and listen to my breath climb
the rungs of my ribs with more
to give this world
than a long cry.

I rise to daylight,
soft and shadowless.
Rocks, too, have turned over.

About the Author

Eleanor Kedney is the founder of The Writers Studio Tucson, a branch of the New York-based creative writing school founded by Philip Schultz, where she served as the director and the advanced workshop teacher for ten years. Her poems have appeared in various U.S. and international periodicals, including *Connecticut River Review, Cumberland River Review, Cutthroat, Many Mountains Moving, Miramar Poetry Journal, Mslexia, Mudfish, NY Quarterly, San Pedro River Review, Skidrow Penthouse, The Maynard,* and several other journals. She has contributed to the anthologies *No Achilles: War Poetry* (WaterWood Press, 2015), *Write to Meow* (Grey Wolfe Publishing, 2015), and *Poems on Loss Anthology* (Little Lantern Press, 2016). She lives with her husband, Peter, their dog, Charlie, and their cat, Ivy, in Tucson, Arizona and Stonington, Connecticut.

Learn more at *www.eleanorkedney.com.*

Acknowledgments

My sincere thanks to the editors of the following publications, in which these poems, some in earlier versions, have appeared:

"My Brother Pruning the Sweet Gum Tree"   *American Poets & Poetry*

"Apple Pie"   *Connecticut River Review*

"Reading Frank O'Hara after My Mother's Death"   *Cumberland River Review*

"Twelve Days from Transfer"   *Many Mountains Moving*

"Shoes"   *Many Mountains Moving*

"After a Death, I Take a Walk"   *Miramar Poetry Journal*

"Between the Earth and Sky"   *Mudfish*

"Movement"   *Skidrow Penthouse*

"Good to See You"   *The Maynard*

Gratitude

I want to express my deepest gratitude to Philip Schultz for his insights, advice, encouragement, and most of all, his belief in me as I worked through this material.

I want to thank Juliet Patterson, who so thoughtfully read and responded to these poems.

I am grateful to the late Richard Dyer-Bennet, the minstrel, who heard the music in my poems and encouraged me as a young poet, and the late Louis Simpson, my first poetry mentor, for his wise counsel and the course he set me upon.

I would also like to thank family, friends, my Writers Studio Tucson students, and fellow Writers Studio teachers, for their support and inspiration.

I'm especially grateful to my mother for her tireless commitment to family. She was my anchor. And, to my father, whose heartfelt letters and postcards to me inspired a love for verse.

To my husband, Peter Schaffer——my rock and shepherd——my heart.

Other Books from Liquid Light Press

All Liquid Light Press books are available directly from
liquidlightpress.com or from any of the current major global
distribution channels including Amazon, Barnes and Noble, the
iBookstore and the Ingram Catalog.

- ♥ *Leaning Toward Whole* by M. D. Friedman (2011) –
  Explores the poignant and personal. Also available as a
  groundbreaking multimedia enhanced e-book.
- ♥ *The Miracle Already Happening – Everyday Life with Rumi*
  by Rosemerry Wahtola Trommer (2011) – A special
  collection of poems full of heart, humor, peace and wisdom.
- ♥ *Spiral* by Lynda La Rocca (2012) – A compelling poetic and
  melodic discourse of the persistent cravings and fears inside of
  each of us.
- ♥ *From the Ashes* by Wayne A. Gilbert (2012) – A true
  masterpiece that gnaws at the heart with universal appeal.
- ♥ *ah* by Rachel Kellum (2012) – This poetry has a simplicity and
  clarity that cuts to the core of being human.
- ♥ *Catalyst* by Jeremy Martin (2012) – *Catalyst* may just launch
  you on a fiery ride into yourself.
- ♥ *Of Eyes and Iris* by Erika Moss Gordon (2013) – Beautiful yet
  poignant in its simplicity.
- ♥ *Your House Is Floating* by Susan Whitmore (2013) – As
  smooth, crisp and satisfying as olive oil on fresh garden greens.
- ♥ *Nowhere Near Morning* by Jeffrey M. Bernstein (2013) –
  An intimate embrace of what it means to be alive.
- ♥ *Harmonica* by Cecele Allen Kraus (2014) – *Harmonica*
  bristles with a shimmering music that heals the heart.
- ♥ *Surf Sounds* by Roger Higgins (2014) – Expertly crafted and
  superbly written, pulsing with the tides of the soul.
- ♥ *Black-Footed Country* by Lindsay Wilson (2015) – Like
  eating an artichoke, there are layers within thorny layers, each
  one more tender and subtle until you feast on the heart inside.
- ♥ *The Dice Throwers* by Douglas Cole (2015) – *The Dice
  Throwers* shines like a flashlight across the gritty dark alleys of
  the American soul, turning shattered glass into diamonds.
- ♥ *Lessons on Sleeping Alone* by Megan E. Freeman (2015) –
  While easily accessible, Megan's elegant writing is complexly
  layered with hard-won common sense and clarity.

www.ingramcontent.com/pod-product-compliance
Lightning Source LLC
Chambersburg PA
CBHW021915040426

42447CB00007B/878